M000032263

WRITERS REPUBLIC

EMBRACING
DAD HABITS

A HANDBOOK FOR EARLY FATHERHOOD
& SOON-TO-BE-DADS

CONLEY PRIMUS

This publication contains the opinions and ideas of its author. It is intended to provide helpful and informative material on the subjects addressed in the publication. The author and publisher specifically disclaim all responsibility for any liability, loss, or risk, personal or otherwise, which is incurred as a consequence, directly or indirectly, of the use and application of any of the contents of this book.

WRITERS REPUBLIC L.L.C.
515 Summit Ave. Unit R1
Union City, NJ 07087, USA

Website: *www.writersrepublic.com*
Hotline: *1-877-656-6838*
Email: *info@writersrepublic.com*

Ordering Information:
Quantity sales. Special discounts are available on quantity purchases by corporations, associations, and others. For details, contact the publisher at the address above.

Library of Congress Control Number: 2020946713
ISBN-13:   978-1-64620-658-2   [Paperback Edition]
                 978-1-64620-699-5   [Hardback Edition]
                 978-1-64620-659-9   [Digital Edition]

Rev. date: 10/05/2020

Contents

Dear Fathers,

Please turn back to the cover of this book and remember that image of Dad very well. I want you to use it as a calming mantra whenever fatherhood gets tough and your days get crazy. Notice in the image, Dad is sitting in tranquility while each of his main and extended hands are preoccupied. Somehow, he's handling multiple aspects of his life while seemingly at peace with himself. This is the state of balance I hope to help you to achieve with this book; finding harmony within the chaos of parenting and manhood. It requires a lot to be a great father, so whenever you're feeling overwhelmed, take a look at that image of Dad; close your eyes and take a deep breath. Be patient.

- The Wrench represents manly duties and leadership responsibility.
- The Bottle represents fatherly compassion, nurturing, and being a guardian.
- The Ring represents love, emotional engagement, and your romantic life.
- The Money reflects your finances, having discipline and patience.
- The Ball reflects your personal interests, hobbies, and self-awareness.
- The Phone represents staying connected with friends and being socially outgoing.

-

1

Introduction
(About the Author)

I want to start by saying; this moment is not about me at all; it's entirely about you. How great you can be, how many flaws you can discover within yourself, and how much of a habit you can make your growth. I've always been the kind of person that wanted to help everybody, even when I needed help myself. My name is Conley but you can call me your brother now that we're in the circle of fatherhood together. I'm a young African American man with a toddler daughter who cares deeply about fatherhood and how it affects the human race.

My parents were born and raised in the Caribbean island of St Vincent before migrating to America in their late 20s. By the time I was 10, my parents had separated and my mother already did the hard work moving my older sister and me into a beautiful home in Brooklyn, New York. I grew up in a sort of luxury but tossed into an environment where other kids taught me more about life in America than my parents ever could. I went through a weird disconnect with my mind and wealth and got consumed with pop culture, fashion, and girls. Most young boys from my neighborhood do. It's a hood where everything should be fun and being cool is the main priority, based on whatever trends are out. One hood I never thought about was fatherhood. I loved kids because I was always a big kid myself, but I never imagined having a kid of my own. After having a lot of ups and downs with the law, girls, and self-discovery, I didn't have a kid until I was 26 years old. I consider that old, coming from the era I came from. The self-discovery was the most important aspect for me because it helped shape who I became as a man. Learning that there's a purpose to life beyond what's taught to us inspired me to realize that everything happens for a reason. This made it extremely easy for me to embrace fatherhood.

I look at everything with sort of a mystical sense, and sometimes it can lead me to overthink. I feel like every man has his own approach to how he views life. Understanding your approach is important to solidifying your confidence as a person. If you can't think deeply about life, you'll miss out on a lot of great lessons other than how to survive or make money. None of these things may appear important when you're a teenager or young adult...but as a father, everything tends to hold some sort of substance. As a newborn grows up, they learn to talk, and their favorite word is "Why?" Ironically, that was one of my favorite words before I ever became a father; and it helped me tremendously. The very first lesson here is; be prepared and learn all that you can. As a father, you'll want to stand out, and have something you can pass on besides physical wealth or DNA.

I've spoken to countless fathers, and a lot of times I find the magical view of life missing from them in their reasoning. I can't really blame them either. The obstacles of life strip away at the smile of a human, to the point where only "adult things" can make them happy; things they wouldn't share with their child. It's important to find substance and happiness in things you would expose your child to. It's the main reason I decided to write this book. I wanted to share my views and what I've learned through countless research and connecting the dots. I've never gone to college, but I've researched the human brain, religions, anatomy, child development, and much more...giving me a different perspective on life than a lot of my peers. I want to share that, especially as a father. A lot of times I see men subconsciously underestimating how important their efforts are to a family. I understand that since men don't get pregnant, it's hard to really connect to their kids the way they're supposed to.

That's why we're here. I want to expose your mind to a few ideas and points of view; facts you may never have considered that might help you get to a mental point of vulnerability needed to grow into a great Father. I've made many mistakes in my lifetime, and my mission now is to make sure my daughter doesn't make those same mistakes in vain. I don't want you making those same mistakes either, because we're all in this together. I also never want to forget that I was a child once and naive enough to make those mistakes. It takes that level of consideration to be a good father, if that's what you want to be. I'm writing this book to make sure all you fathers never pass on your childhood traumas to your kids.

One of my childhood traumas is that my parents never complimented me much. While peers and teachers had a lot to say about the way I thought, my mom and dad always called me smart but never seemed too impressed. As a result, words of affirmation were the greatest thing you can do for me as an adult. I crave hearing how good I'm doing, and sometimes it can backfire. Knowing this allows me to correct these false motivations and not mistakenly deprive my child of endearment. Ultimately, I've realized that most men don't get to a point of emotional self-awareness to even identify that they have childhood traumas in the first place. Knowing that our children have to suffer because we fail to know we have work to do, breaks my heart. Remember, this journey is about you Dad, and I can only use myself as an example.

The main thing you should know about me is that I'm a very spiritual person. I'm not particularly religious, but I believe heavily in the importance of prayer and manifestation; trying to find the meaning of your life, and putting your fate in the power of love.

Unity and togetherness are the only way we can evolve as a species, and that's a principle that I hold dearly in life. In this book, I won't try to push any of my ideas on you, but rather try to bring you to a space where you can be as open-minded as I am, if not more. I want to give you things to consider, ideas to sleep on, and new approaches to apply to not only fatherhood but your life as a man. I'm not perfect, and before you go on any journey, it's important to know that you aren't perfect either. I hope to one day learn from you just like you may learn something here from me. Give yourself room to fail, and more importantly give yourself room to realize when you're failing, and work on having the self-awareness to correct your mistakes after owning them. I believe we're connected to the stars as much as I believe a creator crafted the earth and the entire universe. However, this moment isn't about me. It's entirely about you. What do you believe in? I want you to know you're a brother to me, and your pain is my pain. Your trials and tribulations, every mistake, and every celebration; is also a part of my story. As parents, we are connected as leaders of a new world, responsible for the personalities, experiences, and outcomes of young babies that will grow to be the rulers of this planet. If fatherhood isn't THAT deep to you, allow me to explain to you why it should be. Why you should do the work like a man to heighten your self-awareness and better yourself for your family; for mom, and for your child or children. If mom has already given birth to your baby, congratulations on already doing an outstanding job. If you're still expecting or want to get some insight before you plan on having a baby with your partner, take a moment to realize the fact that you're about to become the most important man in a person's life; a Father. As a part of the parenting brotherhood, it's my duty to share all the knowledge I can with you based on what I've experienced, studied, and applied to my mindset. I wrote this book for all the men who are new fathers or soon to be fathers, that may have heard that they are too "dense" or "insensitive" before. I thank you for reading and remaining open-minded.

Chapter 1:
Welcome to the Real World

The night before your child is born, you're just a Man. Once your partner gives birth, an evolution takes place. You evolve from being a Man to being a Father. As magical as it seems, it isn't magic at all and takes constant growth, effort, and open-mindedness. That fact that you're even reading this proves that you're on the right path; researching and seeking out different advice and perspective about the world of Fatherhood. I want to begin by saying congratulations on joining us in parenthood, and how proud of you I am for taking the extra step as a father. As parents, we all benefit from how much love and effort YOU put into your baby.

Parenting is often referred to as a "thankless job"...and it is. It's more of a job than it is thankless, but it's important to remember that almost the entire world is parenting; in fact, it's been a constant cornerstone in humanity since the beginning of time. I say that to say; parenting may be just as hard as any other part of life but it's almost the point of life. All parents deal with different difficulties, but ultimately there is something sentimental about raising your offspring and passing on your DNA. Amongst basically every species on the planet, continuing your genes seems to be the priority. Parenting is more than a job; it's fundamental... continuing the human race while passing on your traditions, viewpoints, and most importantly your corrected behaviors and protection from the traumas you've had to heal from along the way. It's spiritual and scientific all in one, ancient yet new and unique every single time. It's important to approach being a parent with this mindset at all times. Carefully consider that the things you force your child to experience will evolve with them and go on with them as they assimilate into the world. Always think of that child as half of your essence being passed on; a consciousness that chose you to help it navigate this physical realm together. Fully understanding the purpose of parenthood will help you see your child as a vulnerable ally that's truly depending on you to protect them while preparing them for a world that has very little protection. Parenting on its own is a relentless task that takes patience, planning, empathy, self-reflection, and endurance... but then there's Fatherhood. Fatherhood is much more than being the breadwinner, baby-proofing the house, or putting together high chairs. Parenting is an experience, to say the least, but fatherhood is a beast of its own... something that takes a lot of effort in different elements of life to even begin to master. Remember you're not alone...you can now begin to relate to your parents, neighbors, and peers in ways you could have never imagined. The struggle of breeding life in this chaotic world and raising a living being while still learning to take care of yourself can be an intimidating task, but it creates a sense of unity amongst parents which gives you access to a surplus of advice, ideas, and growth.

I can't ignore just how vital it is to parenting that you've made the right choice on the mother of your child. I don't want to scare you brother, because most fathers reading this book are already invested in the lover that will be or is the mother of their child. However, we'll have to speak on this for a moment, especially for the readers that aren't quite sure about when they'll be a father yet. You'll need to be around a true friend, a partner who can genuinely love you and wish to see you grow. Someone who is kind and wants good things for themselves in life. A lot of people can be stagnant by mistake, and rub that energy off onto others. It's healthy to enter parenthood with someone who is outgoing and understands the importance of learning and intelligence; a woman who works hard and expresses open-mindedness. As a man, it's hard to demand these qualities from someone when you don't display any of them yourself, so I'm here to tell you that you'll need to constantly work on yourself. Once you get a woman pregnant, a small fire starts to burn. For the first time, you and your partner TRULY have to consider 'forever' and what your bond will be like for the rest of your lives. You're now linked forever with a child, a consciousness that you will be fully responsible for a long time. The Fire that starts to burn represents all the good and bad memories you two have, all the good and bad traits you've noticed, embraced, and ignored; exactly how you feel about the way she loves you. All of these elements will begin to matter much more to you, and how a mom reacts to this realization varies depending on the woman. This fire can either become a large, warming light that guides you two through the dark and tough times...or, a blazing disaster that's full of smoke and burned bridges. It's not entirely up to you, but you're an important factor in making the partnership work. The very first step you can take to making parenthood work is understanding yourself as a man and a lover. Knowing what you like, what you lack, and what you need are all important when finding a partner and this also translates to parenting. "Do we work well through issues?" That is probably the first question you want to ask yourself because there will be a plethora of problems the two of you will face as parents traversing this modern society. Some people also heavily consider Genetics (looks, generational ailments, twins in the family) when choosing a partner but I won't get into that. I personally feel like the second most important factor in a partner is their willingness to work for themselves and others; also known as Ambition.

There's an incomparable blessing that comes with parenting, and that is Ambition. From the moment you were born, life has always been about learning. Learning how to have fun, learning how to make friends, learning how to save money, and learning how to take care of yourself. If you have younger siblings or have ever babysat like most people, you've gotten a taste of taking care of a completely dependent bundle of energy. The stakes completely change when the child is your own; and I can't stress that enough. For maybe the first time, life becomes about learning and teaching simultaneously. Surviving the journey of gaining the life you want while building good habits with your baby at the same time WILL exhaust you, so take your diet and routine seriously to maximize your energy.

The more you study and understand diet, food, and energy, the easier it will be for you to decide what kind of dietary approach you'll use with your child too. This is a key factor in parenting that fathers often overlook. Most human adults have very unhealthy eating habits and are addicted to bleached sugars and salts. Think about the REASON humans eat food. It's for nutrients, right? Now, what's the reason YOU eat food? Probably because it tastes good. Allowing our tongue and taste buds to dictate our diets have completely disconnected us from the actual purpose of eating. The bad health effects are so enormous that people often view them as common hurdles of life, like high blood pressure or heartburn. That domino effect sometimes leaves people confused about what's good to eat or not. In our teenage years, we stockpile unhealthy snacks and build a sort of immunity to things like acidity and sugar rushes. This is not the case for a newborn or a toddler. It's crucial to consider what kind of foods you want to feed your child. Veggies and fruits are always a safe idea, as well as sugar and corn syrup free products. If you eat meat, consider what kinds and amounts of meat intake you want your toddler to experience. I highly suggest avoiding BEEF for the first 5 years of a child's life. The amount of nutrients the human body and brain receives is the building block for how a child's motor functions, memory, and energy levels will pan out.

Do you know WHY humans cook our food? It's ancient really, and probably the reason we became so smart. As we know, our digestive systems break down food with stomach acids to give us the nutrients we need to build energy. A part of digesting food is breaking down the atomic molecules it's made out of. Cooking food exposes it to fire where the heat breaks molecules apart and shakes them up (the reason solid ice breaks down into liquid water) into new, looser formations. It literally transforms the chemical structure of the food, which does half the work for our stomachs when we eat it. You can see this for yourself when cooking anything from steaks to carrots. Research suggests that the discovery of cooking our food before we eat it has given the human body so much extra energy and time to focus elsewhere than our stomachs, that it might just be why our brains have grown so much. Interesting, isn't it? The reason we have the largest brains on the planet could possibly be because we're the only species that cooks our food. Food for thought. That being said, your child's diet is almost life-determining in how much energy their brains will have to work on itself, rather than process the harsh gemology of western society. Make sure your baby is eating for nutrients and not for taste. Eventually, your child's body should get exposed to these unavoidable preservatives in most of our foods, but protect their mind, body, and soul for as long as you can.

Diet is energy or lack thereof. I'm not promoting any veganism but I'd suggest avoiding meat at all for the first 2 years of life; and here's why. Think of any animal you like...is it a herbivore, or a carnivore? Imagine the dental structures of carnivores like Tigers, Lions, and Sharks...they all have aggressively sharp and long dental structures for ripping through flesh. They have high bacterial based stomach acids and saliva to match this because meat takes a lot of energy to break down in the digestive system. Herbivores on the other hand have a much different dental structure (think Deer, Rabbits, and Cows) with flat teeth and large stomachs that match their diet. Then there are omnivores like monkeys, apes, and bears (and us!) who are both plant and meat-based; but none of them eat meat in abundance; heavily plant-based diets. It turns out the human body and stomach aren't genetically equipped to break down meat at the capacity in which we eat it. I believe it's best to lean on your species strengths, and humans have only two sharp teeth out of 32 for a reason. Everything in moderation; just a suggestion. As a father, you'll have to be as annoying as I am when it comes to research. Seek out information and try your best to fit learning into your everyday life. Whether it's listening to podcasts or documentaries on your way home from work or reading in your alone time, please find a routine in learning not only about parenting but more about life in general. You won't remember everything you see or hear but feeding your brain and getting it used to listening and learning should be a habit of every man that wishes to be successful. Your mental diet is just as important as what you eat because it will transform the information you can pass on to your child and enhance your ability to communicate with others. I hope by now you already see how seriously I take fatherhood. Don't get me wrong, I've been very laxed in life and haven't always had a clear direction, but I WANT to be better every day. You don't have to consider half the things I do but I beg you to desire to be better my brother.

Overall, now more than ever is the time to truly learn how to look yourself in the mirror as a man and consider how you can be better. You're already a great man, but you can always be a greater father. This is an overwhelming moment in any man's life, and he faces many obstacles as he prepares for fatherhood. It's still a better time than ever to begin a journey that parenthood will force you to start at some point anyway. This journey is trying to understand the purpose of life from your perspective. Being involved in raising a child will begin to drastically change the way you see life. While most of us are consumed by finances, the purpose of life may be buried within all the consistent teachings of the world. Religion, mythology, chakras and meditation, astrology, and science all factor into the meaning of life, and it's best to expand your mind and start to get familiar with all of it because knowledge is power. Not all fathers take this approach to raise a child, but they likely reach a midlife crisis where things come crashing down for them; or worse, they end up raising dysfunctional children. YOU can avoid this. Mental versatility will keep you willing and able to grow and figure out ways to lead in moments where inevitable problems will arise. If all of my suggestions about life seem overwhelming to you, stick to two ideals and study as much as you can to expand your mind. The key to parenting isn't as simple as remaining open-minded, but that is an important factor in learning this new world of responsibility and fatherhood you're in; welcome to the real world.

Chapter 2:
The Chemical Head Start

Men... cannot get pregnant. I know the sentence may seem like a real "duh!" moment, but I need you to understand what it really means. When a woman gets pregnant, her body immediately begins to change. It opens up a portal, in a sense; a new mind, a new life and consciousness enters the world, almost magically. From the proteins in the semen released out of your male body, the mother somehow defies science and hosts a 50% foreign bodily entity for almost a year. Many of her bones thin to create new blood at a high rate to share with the baby as it grows and almost all of her blood vessels widen to help pass oxygen, sugar, proteins, and several nutrients to the fetus. All of these processes also release hormones that swiftly change her moods and thoughts as a side effect. Her lungs, heart, stomach, liver, kidneys, intestines, and ribs all move upwards, cramming into her upper torso to help make space for her growing uterus. While all of this happens, every single cell in her body; including her brain cells, are all evolving inside her to prepare for motherhood. A prime example of this is Breast Milk. If an infant is sick or ill in any sort of way, the nipples of the mother (or any woman who has recently given birth) can analyze the saliva of the child and instantly add the needed protein and antibodies to the breast milk to help the child combat the virus. Did you know that? While the entire mind, body, and soul of a woman are affected by sharing her mortality with another thinking, living soul; then there are dads. Little to nothing biologically happens to men as they prepare for Fatherhood. If he's invested, a man's sheer thoughts and stress can force his body to give off similar symptoms to pregnancy like a vast appetite or extreme fatigue. Other than that, Men have no help from science and must find time to plan ahead, in between rightfully catering to an ever-changing attitude of a woman they most likely love.

Not only must you supply emotional security, you must find a way to allude confidence and give mental security in an environment you both are completely new to. Mom will never consider the insanity it might put you through, and she shouldn't or more so doesn't have time to when trying to prepare for a life change while dealing with hormones. So, it's important to have reliable friends or associates to vent to; just remember you're always going to be wrong so never seek some sort of validation. If you believe you're already a hard-nosed kind of guy, this won't be much of an issue. However, if you're more on the emotionally aware side, it's better to learn how to take things on the chin early. DO NOT TAKE THINGS PERSONALLY. Constantly remind yourself that you guys are a team, and you're the only one at 'full strength'. If you're into sports, think of it as an injured star player suiting up in the Finals game 7 to help you, their other star, win a championship ring. Every error they make, you'll have to feel a little bad and understand the effort no matter how badly you want to win. In this situation, YOU will have to play harder AND smarter to win. If you get wrapped up in being angry at their errors, you'll lose focus and absolutely lose the game. Easier said than done, but you'll have to do whatever it takes to make it happen as a team. Keep in mind; she was a star before the "injury". If done correctly, being a father 'dealing with' pregnancy is a perfect moment to bond with the mother. This is a special moment because it will create a bond you may never get the chance to create again. Showing your resiliency and learning to literally be there for her in her darkest mental moments; even as the enemy sometimes; will show your partnership and manhood in a whole new light and establish respect that's crucial for fatherhood in early parenthood.

Every mother is different, and every pregnancy is different, as well as the situation. What remains the same in every family dynamic is how greatly imperative it is to have a good FRIENDSHIP with the mother of your child, and how immensely it plays into the relationship you'll be able to establish with your newborn. Yes, I know, I know...I haven't touched on financial security as yet, right? That may be the most daunting part of parenting, even if you're already financially established. It's a hard situation to speak on because while finances vary vastly amongst readers, the need for more sources of income is always present. If your newborn isn't here yet, the most important advice I've ever got on this topic is "you'll never feel like your pockets are ready for a kid". And that's proven true for me. The key is to not overreact. Your mind can become flustered the minute you find out you're going to be a father, and that's okay. Just remember you need to research, organize, budget, and most importantly communicate your plans to the mother of your child.

Always be accepting of her boundaries but trust your vision no matter how combative she may seem. This is because a woman goes through THREE different periods of pregnancy called Trimesters, all with different effects on the woman's diet, growth, and hormones. During the second trimester (4-6 months pregnant), hormones are at their peak and can become so raging that mothers can find themselves even angrier because they're angry for no apparent reason. Because their moods change so swiftly, they tend to self-reflect a lot and can become really apologetic and affectionate after disagreements; as long as you don't push back against their hormonal moments. It's important to move gracefully and never seem like your uninvested BECAUSE you know she has "raging hormones", but also never become too invested that you seem to suggest what they're saying or doing is irrational. As long as you remain solid, she will realize her faults on her own soon enough. To be honest, you don't have the time and energy to spare on arguing with your partner, especially during pregnancy.

Stick to your vision and remember the keyword for getting your finances in order is "Saving". It's time to fall back on a lot of habits and hobbies that may expense you. You'll have to get used to eating lighter and hanging out less, which should be encouraged by your partner since she'll need your presence for constant care and assistance. Being present at home will be much easier than trying to avoid eating a lot. As mom gets further into her pregnancy, her appetite will balloon and her taste buds will expand. She may be interested in foods and flavors she didn't enjoy before, like spicy foods or weird combinations. Oftentimes you'll find yourself tempted to eat with her, especially since being her aide exhausts a lot of your energy. Try to fight against this and get the cheapest things on the menu if you must; it's crucial to smart a routine to save money. I suggest starting off on a weekly cycle of adding; let's say $20 to a savings. Each week, double the amount of money you put into savings until the end of the month (week one is $20, week two will be $40 and then $80 on week 3). At the end of the month, you'll have $300 saved where you can reset your deposit if you want. By the time 9 months pass; you'll have $2,700 saved up. It's a start, and if you have the means to put more money into the pot to start, Do it. For context, using this technique will save you $3,600 in a year. It's easier said than done and takes lots of discipline, but remember you don't have a chemical head start and owe all the effort to your family.

These mental hurdles will continue after the child is born as well, because 9 months is never the end of pregnancy. You now have a newborn that won't sleep throughout the night for about three months. You also have the woman you love recovering from hosting the child as all her organs drop slowly back into place; releasing a surplus of hormonal mood swings yet again.

Immediately following the birth of your child, mom will be blessed with a special kind of breast milk called 'Colostrum'. Most new moms learn about this through books or the nurses at the hospital but you need to know as well. Colostrum is breast milk that has heavy protein concentrations that pass along antibodies to your newborn to fight off diseases; a kind of vaccination that the female body puts together after the trauma of giving birth. Speak with your partner about it in regards to breastfeeding, and even if she elects not to, please convince her to at least pump for the first two weeks so that your baby may ingest Colostrum. Bringing it up might also serve as a plus since it looks like Dad is doing his research.

Some, if not most women will go through moments where they realize their bodies may be changed forever. How to deal with this differs depending on the woman and that's why it's a plus to have a strong friendship and know your partner. If you plan to reassure her that she's still beautiful and desirable, you ALMOST have the right idea. You'll need to understand that your words and actions cannot change what she feels, and what she sees. She's known her body all her life, and these changes, whether it be weight, stretch marks, or something else; can serve as trauma for a moment that has altered what she always knew about herself. Be considerate when being there for her in times of physical self-consciousness. Once you become a father, you'll be tossed into the ring of taking care of two beings. This is a fight that will never stop, and if you love your child, you'll do the hard work of learning how to never make the mother feel less special than the child while simultaneously making your child feel like the most special thing in the world. If you've thoroughly considered the chemical head start a mother gets for parenting, then you'll start to grasp the real extensive work it takes in being a Father. Always be open to learning, and never beat yourself up for not being perfect. It's good to remind yourself that while the days are long, these moments won't last forever. Mom may never get used to the changes her body went through, but her organs will heal, her hormones will stabilize, and her motherly instincts will have her glowing. Be sure to plan with her and get back to the romantic side of your relationship, making her feel loved and youthful. Get to know this motherly version of your partner because there are subtle changes; notice her priorities and make sure you help out by changing some diapers! As the newborn grows into an infant and soon a toddler, it'll be apparent that the relationship the parents have MUST grow every day as well. If you haven't noticed by now, all the questions you've ever had about the relationship that you've buried in the back of your mind will have to remain there forever and die. This is because it's time to acknowledge that whatever relationship you and the mother have will be forever; and there's a new bundle of joy you'll need to help her raise, forever. Whatever thoughts you have moving forward, consider your child, consider the mother, and consider 'forever'. While these early stages of parenting are stressful, don't make the mistake of thinking the head start a mother gets lasts forever. Understand that while a woman may be able to tell you what she needs from you as a man, no woman or child will be able to explain to you what they need from you as a Father. It is entirely on you to try your best and fill in all the gaps. You always want the aspire to be better for yourself, most importantly. Being driven by wanting to support your family is natural, but you may find yourself taking things too personal if you depend on loved ones to fuel you. This is all a part of your chemical process, and it starts with the mental work. Training your mind to want to be the best over any other temporary emotions or misunderstandings is key to your growth as a Father. You'll find that many problems you have to protect your child from will come in the form of other adults, and you don't want to include emotions like anger, revenge, or confusion in your decision making. It's extremely difficult to let go of issues in real time when emotions and tension are high. So it's good to get a head start on having conversations with yourself and prepping your mind to stay rational.

Another common struggle fathers deal with (especially with new mothers) is being pushed into a secondary role as a parent. A lot of times it will seem difficult because of the sheer physical labor you shoulder during the earliest years of your child's life. Your financial inputs will be viewed as normality and your efforts will be minimized a lot, as well as your decisions with the child. This is normal, mainly because Mom just spent 9 long months risking her life for this new bundle of joy.

The umbilical connection a mother and her child have will be irreplaceable, and oftentimes it leads mothers to force patterns and habits on a father that leaves him used to being unengaged. This is a harmful cycle because fathers can be stuck in a space where they leave the "motherly tasks" to their partner while she aggressively seeks his help. For example, women can become very territorial with things like baby outfits, hairstyles or picture themes. Fathers sometimes don't see the big deal in these things and decide to leave those choices up to her. Over time, it can become overbearing for mom and she'll look to you for help. Chances are she won't ASK for help because you're the father and you already have to parent the same child. Unfortunately, mom won't consider that she just spends a lot of time pushing a new father into a bubble of feeling like he's less important of a parent than her, or that he cannot make decisions for his child without running them by her in gatekeeper fashion.

The best way to avoid this cycle is by preparing for it, and understanding that new mothers may have an abundance of help from their bodies, but they're still fairly new to understanding how to raise a newborn with the man they love. In a sense, she is right; she has the breast milk, blood plasma connection, and familiar heartbeat; a rhythm your newborn has been listening to with vibrations since before their ears developed. She is physically far more important than you, but as a Father, you should never get into a mindset of branching off gender roles for parenting. Make sure not to find yourself being petty when your partner begins to ask for your opinion, because she's also new to being a parent. This is empathy, and an important part of being a cohesive team. Take the initiative to be an active father early on starting with basic bonding techniques like skin-to-skin time with your baby and rocking them to sleep in your arms for nap time. Get down on the ground with them as they learn to crawl and walk, entering a world from their point of view. Learn to practice be caring, compassionate, confident, and forgiving as a person because the chemical "head start" mom has evens out once your baby is around two years old, and your bond will be apparent (no pun intended). Patience is the key. We live in a hard-wired, fast-paced world where we take risks and enjoy instant pleasure. We as men aren't typically built to have patience and often lose our tempers. Without patience, there is no self-control or discipline and that means there is no manhood. Patience with the mother of your child or your partner is a necessity for a healthy family, and it will also prepare you for the excessive amount of patience needed to keep up with your child experiencing life for the first time.

Chapter 3:
Alien Experience

A baby comes into this world knowing nothing. It's something you hear all the time, to the point it's become sort of a phrase. I personally believe this is far from the truth. No matter what your belief is about our existence, you have to admit that there is some cool magic to having a baby. From a small army of proteins in your scrotum, this LIFE is born within the mother. A cluster of neurons in the brain creates this complex form of awareness that we call consciousness. It controls the motor functions of breathing (where did lungs even come from?) and all the senses, learning and feeling pain and hunger over and over again. I like to call this unexplainable awareness a "Soul". It's important to think deeply about humanity and your link to your child because it will better your commitment as a father. Being responsible for a new soul can be very intimidating but if done confidently, you can unlock a whole new passion for life that seemingly feels necessary to understand your true purpose. Earlier, I called birth a sort of 'portal'. I like to think, is there a life for a soul before it forms into a fetus? It's a question we may never know the answer to...and if you're religious you may be familiar with the idea of souls coming from a sort of Heaven, to have a human experience. It's fair to say that if you had a life before this one, you'd remember it, right? Yet how can that be true if you don't even remember your own birth? It's a divine thought and really makes you wonder. If we turn to the very ancient teachings of Astrology and the Zodiac, we find that the entire personality of a person can be estimated by their date and time of birth. It suggests that our "souls" are somehow connected to planetary bodies surrounding our Sun. The zodiac remains both controversial and respected in our times, so it's up to you if you consider it a thing. Just ask yourself, "Why do I know my zodiac sign if it's such a far-fetched idea?" What I'm trying to say is that learning a child can seem like an impossible situation to navigate. They can't speak until you teach them; after their tongues have developed. They can't walk or eat properly for a while and they can't understand their own emotions, making them irritable and exhausting at times. What's interesting through all of this, is that your child learns everything it can from you, but develops a personality of their own seemingly out of nowhere. Traits like bravery, curiosity, shyness, and determination can be spotted very early in the infant stage of a child, and these are traits that can stick throughout the life of a person unless some sort of trauma or restraint is put on them by the parent or other adults. It's very important to learn the characteristics of your child as they grow into their own little person.

Researching body language and early childhood tips can help you grasp the struggles your child may be facing without being able to express it yet. Keep in mind that YOU are responsible for many of the behaviors your child will pick up when it comes to expression. I'll be reminding you this often, because a lot of parents don't realize it. If kids yell when they're frustrated, or dance when they're happy; all of this will reflect how you express yourself around them. Your self-awareness is vital here because you will need to spot situations where you're responsible for the child's incorrect expression and not punish them for innocently reflecting your bad habits. These are moments where you become a team, taking the moment to teach your toddler and yourself about the right and wrong about a situation. Speaking simple lessons about emotions that you struggle to follow will help you better apply it to yourself, and be a better person and parent for your child. Respect your child. This means understanding at all times that they do not exactly know what their emotions are or mean, but this does not mean they are foolish. Children spot patterns and have a high rate of memory. They can take advantage of your caring nature but it's toxic as a parent to assume a new soul understands everything they are doing. Be sure to use any and every scolding moment as a time to explain Who, What, Where, When, and Why they are wrong, or right for how they've handled a situation or expressed themselves. It's healthy to establish routines for yourself and your child that includes learning, activity, senses stimulation, and nap time. Use any and every moment to teach your child whatever information you may know. While babies are adorable and soft, it's good to speak clearly and firmly. As your baby learns to speak, stress the idea pronouncing their words fully. The brain always looks for shortcuts and children tend to ramble through sentences and get used to pronouncing words the wrong way. Make them feel comfortable at all times but express your language clearly and be a good example of never being afraid to speak. Children need to be confident that their parents are an ally and a friend. Some parents may think you shouldn't be friends with your child, but that's because they look at parenthood as a job. In a job setting, this is true, a CEO should never do the work of a janitor, and all titles have different levels. I know we've said before that fatherhood is like a thankless 'job' but this isn't how parenting works.

Parenthood is more like building a house. Friendship is always a core ground level of any house; the basement. As you build floors on top of the basement you establish being a protector, provider, teacher, guardian, and lastly you get to the attic, which is being a Father. You'll have access to every room from the attic to the basement and can remain flexible to be any safe space your child needs. It's critical to figure out how to be a friend and a guardian.

You can mirror this mindset in your love life as well. You'll want your toddler to never be afraid of admitting they're wrong, but embarrassed at their own actions and able to understand their mistakes. Once an infant reaches 6 months, growth becomes rapid and you'll begin to notice a personality forming. Pay attention to how they like to play, what colors and sounds attract them; what makes your child laugh or seemingly upset. It's vital to create a plan with the mother for establishing a nap system for your baby. Suggestively two naps a day through their first year or two of life. This is because sleep is an important factor to memory. An infant's brain absorbs so much that it needs to wait until most bodily functions are slower in sleep mode to process information and flush useless data. Be consistent in teaching colors, shapes, numbers, and letters to your child no matter how gifted they may seem. Repetition is key to helping the brain realize what's important in this world.

Why is repetition so important? It's because of the way the brain operates and processes information. For example, a toddler brain will link together the fact that if you flip a light switch, the light bulb in the ceiling will illuminate. The brain is like a rainforest cluttered with sensory stimulation and new data. Images of a light switch and a bulb are at different parts of the rainforest and need to cram through a density of scattered information to be linked together. These images are like boulders, slowly creating a path through an entangled forest as they roll until they collide. The more these thoughts meet each other through repetition, the smoother the pathway becomes for the images to link and suddenly your baby understands that if they desire light, a simple act of flipping the switch is needed. This process for the early brain shapes the willingness to learn because repetition builds the mental pathways your baby needs. Think of the brain as an entity that relies on the body and 5 senses to tell it how to survive. Take the time to teach about anything, from materials like wood and plastic to weather systems and how cars move. Don't be afraid to admit you don't know something, or use the chance to look it up together. Technology is a huge part of today's world and it's safe to introduce things like keyboards and touchscreens to your child after a year and a half of hands-on learning with more basic information. Be passionate about learning what your child likes because it can be helpful with teaching them things. Some toddlers like to try tasks themselves, while some like to be shown how to do it. It's easier understanding how to approach a child that can't speak, so things can go smoother and extra emotions won't rile up and blur their concentration. As your child nears the age of 3, they've become a lot more active and vocal. If you've used a pacifier with your child, it's best to come together with mom and make a plan to get the child off the pacifier before the age of 3, the absolute latest (and that's pushing it). You don't want to create a habit of dependency at a stage where the child's brain is developed enough to feel a sort of addiction. Teething is the first time a child's teeth begin to grow visibly from under their gums. It's painful and causes seemingly random outbursts from your baby so it can be a hard time for parents to deal with. This is the moment when children usually get stuck on pacifiers, so I suggest an assortment of teething toys, bibs, and blankets to use instead. Another key element of fatherhood is to always stroke the imagination of your child. Try your best to pay attention to the shows they watch. Learn the names of the main characters and notice their favorite ones. It's helpful to pay attention to the programs and invest in the episodes, getting a refreshing childhood lesson on how to share or help others. This can help you follow up on these lessons in real-life situations and also gain ideas for new ways to engage your child.

I know this can be extremely hard to balance with your personal life, especially with having to provide emotional, financial, spiritual, and physical security for your partner. The main thing you should focus on is Discipline. It's one of the hardest things to acquire but it's a necessity not only for fatherhood but for life itself. It's hard work but worth it for your child, yourself, and everyone who loves you. Discipline can translate into other areas like routine, planning, decision making, and budgeting finances;

all of which will help you be a better overall man. The beauty of this experience is that it's a learning and teaching moment on a constant basis. Mentally it can be exhausting, but that's why you must be consistent. The mind is a muscle. If you keep skipping workouts, the weight may never seem easier to handle. If you keep working at it, things get easier on the mind, and clarity happens. Clarity is almost impossible to see coming, so you must take the steps to discipline yourself so you may begin to see how easy it truly is when you WANT to be better. A perfect way to help bring clarity and discipline to yourself is through exercise. Creating small moments throughout the day where you can work up a sweat and get your heart pumping will help open up your mind in ways I can hardly explain. I'll speak more on staying active later on, but any health or fitness guru will tell you the same; please give it a try and see for yourself.

To master any sort of discipline, you have to have self-awareness and take fatherhood seriously. Every little thing matters, and I'll give you an example from my journey as a dad. I HATE bugs. It's not a fear, but I don't like seeing them crawling or flying around me. My daughter on the other hand? She likes bugs. Specifically, ants and fireflies. She loves to hold fireflies and watch them glow in her hands. Of course, I want no parts of this... but in those moments I realize that I cannot exude discomfort because I am leading her. She's already conquered this idea of insects that I haven't, and it's my duty as a Dad to never bring her vibrations down. Instead, she brings my levels up and I catch fireflies for her. Within that moment, we're a team. I'm helping her learn about and enjoy an amazing flashing spectacle of nature while she helps me on my journey of not hating bugs. This starts with the adult accepting the child as a friend, someone they can learn from. It's a simple thought, but most parents don't have it which traumatizes kids and always comes back to bite the parents.

The most confusing part of raising a kid is understanding that teaching them how to live is not teaching them life. I'll go out on one of my crazy moments but stick with me. Consider this;

27

children born in 250 BC were probably taught to hunt and sword-fight at an early age. Children born in the 1600s were probably taught how to sail and mine at an early age. Murder or operating machinery are useful for surviving life in their times, but it's far from the key to life. You'll need to practice critical thinking, and form an understanding of what life means to you. When you strip away all man-made things, what is the purpose? And how can you express that to your child without deciding the purpose of life for them? Tough decisions that are almost solely on the Father to make; you can find yourself feeling like a new person in sort of an alien experience with completely new priorities to life. Make sure you learn yourself as much as you learn your child.

During the early stages of an infant's life, it's important to be involved as much as you can and not let work consume you. Keep in mind that this is also an alien experience for the Mother of the child as well. Parenting is already a new experience for Mom, but you have to always consider the fact that she is confused by her brand-new mindset as a mother. Her body spends almost a year healing from pregnancy, and some mental hurdles are unfamiliar for her. Spiritually, she may be feeling like a sort of new person, with the sole purpose and responsibility of keeping a baby alive that she just risked her life to give birth to. This is uncharted territory and you want to be sure to be there for her in all the ways you can. Because of these experiences she's dealing with, you cannot expect empathy from her on a deep level, because theoretically, you're more mentally stable to deal with the burden of emotional strain from this new parenting situation than she is. Once your newborn is nearing a year of life, it's detrimental that you and mom have grandparents or close family and friends you can trust to watch them for even a few hours, to lift some mental and physical stress off you and your partner. Alone time to gather your thoughts and feel like yourself will be important through the beginning years of fatherhood, so please try and establish a sort of trust system as early as you can. It helps to make sure your newborn knows these other guardians from a very young age and becomes familiar with their voices and faces. You want your baby to have as many healthy relationships as possible, and being comfortable is fundamental for a human being that can't yet speak. As far as building on the alone time with your partner, I have four familiar words of advice; "Don't take it personal". It generally depends on the woman, but things may get sarcastic, moody, or depressing when it comes to dealing with the hormonal changes mom's body is dealing with. So many mutations are happening in her brain, digestive system, and blood vessels that it's hard to gauge how she's viewing the world or if she may have changed at all; sometimes even permanently. Statistically, many young relationships tend to end after a baby enters the equation. It's mainly because both parents have to consider each other as a true 'life partner' for the first time, but breaking up your family is something you want to avoid at all costs if you love your child. That being said, you never want to lead yourself into depression by staying in a relationship with the wrong person; and a changing spouse can put you in sort of an alien situation again. After practicing self-awareness, trust yourself to make the decision that's best for your family. Account for the fact that while the best decision for you may not be the best decision for your family, you still represent your family, and your top priority should be your child. So please try everything in your power to remain confident and reserve good energy for your partner and baby.

Chapter 4:
Returning to Balance

A s you may have started to realize, life is deep. Parenting is just as deep. It may seem simple within the fact that so many people in the world have been parents...but think of how chaotic the world has been. It's because not everyone has taken parenting as seriously as you. Not everyone is interested in doing research or trying to learn about themselves from a different perspective. As an adult, the one thing you cannot control in parenting is the other adult. Mom's mental journey and understanding of life as well as her acceptance of her role as a parent will rely entirely on her. As a protector and provider, you play a detrimental role in helping her in as many ways as you can, but please understand she has genetically become somewhat of a new person. As I said before, pregnancy has affected her every neuron...and even though she'll be the woman you've always loved, her mind has very much evolved. Whether that be for better or for worse is based on how you approach the situation. If you aren't as serious about your baby as she is, there will be problems. Take accountability for your mistakes but ground yourself in the fact that you cannot and should not want to change who your partner is. These are all decisions you should have sat with before pregnancy, and your child has no time for uncertainty in such a rapid environment. Rely on using your growth as an example for both the child and the mother. Take the word 'leader' seriously and understand there is a cause and effect for every reaction you face. Don't find yourself skipping steps and giving yourself more work by damaging the bond you have with the partner you're going to be raising your child with. This leads me to a point that most men don't want to hear, and some women don't realize we need it. Men need to get more in tune with their femininity. I know it sounds weird, given the fact that women and all their traits have been deemed inferior in society. The jig is up though. A woman's freedom to be moody, change her mind, or be justified in how she feels is part of what makes her human. It's what makes her compassionate and loving, a great leader and an emotionally intelligent being.

Although men pick on women for it, their ability to be themselves in dramatic fashion is what gives them the personality to connect with their inner child and be much more successful as an understanding person than men. In fact, men only pick on them for it because men do not have the freedom to be this way, in a sort of jealous sense. To add insult to injury, living in a male-dominated society suggests that these personality issues men face are self imposed. In a sense, men aren't raised incorrectly. We learn to be tough and strong, never appear confused or intimidated, and to never get too high or low. This is ideal for the world we live in, given the competitive nature and patriarchy of men being the head of the household physically, financially and spiritually. However, all of these things disconnect men from their emotions and feeling them, processing them correctly; all of which is vital to being a healthy human being. Here's a phrase you always hear, "Men don't cry". It means men aren't supposed to show sadness, fear, regret, or any emotion that may lead to tears. Now think of this... WHY DO emotions lead to tears? Like, what science makes these sad, low vibrational emotions lead to fluids excreting out of the tear ducts in your eyes? WHY? And what are emotions anyway; that they translate to physical reactions like sweat and tears? Crying is a weird function, but it's a function nonetheless. It releases something from your body for whatever reason. Think of a bodily function that we understand completely; like farting! Your food breaks down in the acids which create gases your body has to release. That's pretty simple...but imagine holding THAT bodily function in. What effect would that have on your body? Tons. So, the question is, what effects does hold in tears have on your body and emotions? Probably tons. The moral of the story is, men should cry. Feel pain, be confused, and have healthy human moments. If you feel like you can't express these to your partner for whatever patriarchy-of-communication driven reason, find both men and women friends to speak with that you trust. As your communication skills get better, it's very important to find the courage to speak with your partner about your vulnerabilities. It's good to get to know yourself on an emotional level. If it's new to you, it can be terrifying and take a lot of accountability. It's healthy to be able to disappoint yourself and tell yourself you're wrong. It allows you to master empathy and put yourself in others' shoes.

Grasping the lesson that you should never let anyone's evils dictate your charity will help you be a better man, father, and teacher to your child. Emotional awareness will actually allow you to feel what your child feels, through understanding how they react; what soothes them, and what inspires them. Being able to understand yourself means you can better explain yourself to your child and be much more confident in your vision with your partner. I'm not asking you to paint your nails or do your eyebrows; because femininity is much deeper than social norms. Women have the freedom of duality, and those greatest women you know probably have a firm understanding of men because their duality is strong. You too can acquire this ability to be transparent and understand yourself and others better by tapping into your intuition. Workout often and mediate when you can, thinking of soft and calming places. Having trust in yourself will allow your child to trust you, and build on seeing you as more than just a friend, protector and provider; but as a teammate. This may seem biased since I have a daughter, but even with your son you should display a sense of compassion that can open up awareness for a young boy as well, and break the cycle of self-destructive emotional habits expected from males. This also corrects the stigma of fathers subconsciously being harsher with boy toddlers to toughen them up; allowing you to understand how to instill love and affection while also exerting the confidence needed for a growing boy. Duality. Showing respect to and speaking calmly with your partner will also set an example for your son or daughter alike, so your compassion needs to be organic. Another grand step to fatherhood is understanding your metamorphosis. While moms may be rightfully trying to recapture moments of her pre-parent lifestyle, it's best you get used to the idea of spending less time on habits that don't bring in any financial gain. Things like gaming, fishing, camping etc. can seem like part of your personality and hard to let go of, feeling like you're losing yourself. You're actually evolving. Take these moments to reorganize your time and prioritize who you're becoming. In other words, make a hobby out of being a better guardian and provider for your family each day. This growth does not make you less of who you are, because now your child is part of who you are. Attention will naturally go to your family and you won't be able to invest in your hobbies for a while regardless. Be ready to approach this dynamic with a positive mindset of growth and attention to detail, instead of feeling like you're losing yourself in a sort of crisis.

Challenge yourself to explore new talents and lean on your toddler to teach you interesting ways to approach new situations; something they do for a living. Getting to understand your femininity means learning to master traits like gentleness, empathy, humility, and sensitivity. A big mistake you don't want to make is applying too much of these elements to your decision making. You do not want to become overly expressive and emotional, or petty and argumentative with the mother of your child. Getting to know yourself more on an emotional level will lead you to be more expressive, but make sure you sustain your assertiveness and leadership traits. You're still a man and a father who will be relied on to supply direction and protection, so it's best to learn your partner and keep a good balance on masculine and feminine energy. I suggest keeping a sort of journal where you can write down your thoughts, whether it is about old memories you have or complaints about the way life is going. As a father, you'll need to vent and as a man, venting may be a foreign concept to some people. As I said before, society molds men not to be too emotional, shut up, and keep their heads high. It's unhealthy not to vent, so be vulnerable and understand that there are people that relate to how you feel in both high and low moments. Just like tears, releasing your bothersome thoughts is a necessary release. Venting and putting your thoughts into sentences will help you better understand yourself, which helps you to not take things personally since your confidence will be unflappable. Knowing yourself is to know you always have work to do, so no one should be able to tell you that you aren't working. Once you make a habit of venting freely either vocally or in your journal, many things won't haunt you and you'll be able to think and love a lot more clearly.

As your child gets older and older, you probably won't notice that you're paying more attention to their age process than your own. It's easy to lose track of time and get consumed with raising your baby, feeling like the years are passing you by. Other fathers and peers of yours may not be as invested as you are in your child's life, which can add to the idea that you're missing out on things when you see them being social on their own. While I've mentioned before that it's positive to ease up on old hobbies, you should find a way to remain social. Human contact is a key to our life force, and losing out on sunlight and not spending time with others can lead to depression quickly. Mom will be rewarded with tons of social time for going through months of pregnancy, labor, and post-recovery. Dad on the other hand should utilize social media and your phone to communicate with friends. Celebrate your small victories by being social with your friends and even incorporate your child and children of your fatherhood peers into your social activities. Finding ways to be social can always give your child a chance to be outgoing, friendly and daring. Having a shy child is common, as the world can be very aggressive and confusing; but you always want to be a bridge your child can trust to be with in social settings. Try not to scold them embarrassingly, because they won't understand the emotions of "embarrassment" they're feeling. Being in tune with yourself will help establish a leadership role with your child based on trust and not fear. As a man, you have strength in your touch and power in your voice. Your child recognizes and respects that already, every time you lift them into the air or raise your voice when they're doing something dangerous; they recognize your fatherly leadership. It's best to mold that into trust so that in return, your child can be more transparent with you. A mother will most times raise a child within the fact that she went through a lot of pain and risks to bring it into the world. Stick to your own style of parenting brother, because dad is special.

As a father, you need to maintain love with your toddler that makes them not want to disappoint you. As you learn about emotions each day and self-reflect, please take moments to explain emotions to your child as well. You'll be better able to identify how they're feeling when they can't exactly explain it. Toddlers tend to erupt when too many feelings like jealousy, embarrassment, fear, excitement or nervousness clutter their thoughts. Their adrenaline spikes and sometimes it's hard to understand why they're even crying or upset. If you're able to identify their emotions, you can add words to their feelings for them, and explain what it means and how normal it is to experience it as a human. Remember, they're an alien. At first, it won't seem to have any effect explaining emotions to your toddler. But over time, you'll begin to notice that they can recognize when they're frustrated or nervous on their own, and either express that to you before becoming flustered or correcting themselves all on their own. It's an amazing thing to see your child deal with entire self-issues on their own and really understand what it means to be alive. It will translate to the social world for them, as they go to school and retain friendships with recurring faces. Their personalities will blossom and you'll know that as a father you took rightful responsibility in helping them process their emotions. There's no shame in the fact that you're learning every day just like your child is. That is why they're a part of your team after all; to teach you new things about yourself.

Chapter 5:
Twice A Child

Growing up, my father always had a funny saying that goes "Once a Man, Twice a Child". It means that you're in the prime of your life one time. You should own these twilight years where you're both young in mind, body and spirit but old and legal in the eyes of society. "Once a Man" means you're on limited time when you're at your sharpest and growing higher into your potential with each year. "Twice a Child" is the funny part of the phrase though. It means that at the beginning of life, you're in a state where you need help from others and have a harder time grasping the things going on in the world. As you get older and get deeper into your senior years, you'll return to that state although you'll be much wiser. Physically and mentally, you'll need help keeping up with your habits and the evolutions of the outside world. My father always used that phrase to warn me that I shouldn't waste my wonder years on complacency; sometimes I did anyway. As a father myself now, I cannot waste energy or time on things that don't benefit me. I'm usually a fast learner and extremely hands-on, but it took me a long time to fully understand what needed to be done to be a better father and leader for my family. For me, you aren't truly a man until you've become a father. "Once a Man, Twice a Child" has a whole different meaning for me. I see it as; once you're a man (a father), you'll become a child all over again. You're in a brand-new world every single day, learning and barely sleeping; facing new obstacles and figuring out new ways to do tasks better. You're like a child all over again when you're a new Father and having to understand your role can overwhelm all your senses. The key to overcoming this is actually embracing that child-like wonder. Be fascinated with your baby's development daily, and indulge in learning with them. You may know all your basic colors and shapes, but there's much more to learn as your baby grows older into their toddler years, and you should genuinely let your imagination take over. Again, it can be overwhelming being a vulnerable new father who is a stern leader and gentle child simultaneously, and balancing this duality can be easier if you include mom in playtime to build family routines; research fun or developmental activates online specifically for children around the age range of your baby, and get as much rest as you can.

Parenthood is an alliance of superheroes that get to do anything, except sleep. Sleep is important to the human body no matter how old or young you are. As a father, I have lots of trouble with sleep. I wouldn't dare give up my few free hours of my time when my toddler is asleep...and at night time that's when all my ideas flood before I have to sleep for work. I have an issue with sleep. My only hope is keeping myself young in other ways; tapping into my inner child. Having a parent is the greatest thing a child can have...but having a big brother is even cooler. As an adult, we've gone through many, many episodes of life, from falling off a bike to high school bullying and being late for work, and even seeing your favorite woman having a baby. Life shapes us to be moody, grumpy, resilient hardheads. Most adults are far removed from who they truly were as a child. It's kind of silly to expect someone to remain how they were as a child, but outside of adapting to survival, it's the most natural they'll ever be. I believe kids are more soul than flesh. They feel things much more than we do. "Kids see ghosts," they say, and ghosts are supposedly made out of the same energy that drives human beings; frequency. If you're new to the word frequency, it's basically vibrational waves that are released from the electromagnetic energy your body builds up. Think back to your days as a kid when television had those long metal antennas. Whenever the TV was fuzzy and you grabbed the metal rod with your hand, it would normalize the frequency and clear up the picture until you let go again. This is an example of humans having a frequency.

Kids vibrate on a high frequency, and they can feed off of your vibrations as well. It's best to keep your spirits high and try to be as childlike as possible when the time calls for it. Play with your toddler as much as you can. Dressing up, make-belief, and using toys to quiz and teach new things are great ways to bend the imagination and drill real facts into their head. It's surprisingly easier to understand your child when you're thinking like a child. Obviously, you remain an aware adult, but rekindling your childlike spirit will help you understand some of your kid's decisions before they even act them out. Engaging in what they watch is a great way of tapping into your child side. Revisit the cartoons you watched as a kid as well. Remain active with your child and do lots of running, jumping, and lifting with them. This generates a bond with the child that will lead to respect for you and understanding that you always move with their best interest at heart. Keep an eye and ear out for different local activity clubs in your neighborhood and utilize their resources on fun Dad Dates. Taking children swimming as early as newborns is a great and highly recommended activity to invest in since it exercises muscles, regulates bodily gases which lower stress, and enhances cardiovascular fitness for both you and your baby shark. For you, staying active with your child literally keeps you young. The hormones that help your organs stay healthy is referred to as the "youth gene". Scientists have found that this gene is generated from natural impact against your bones from walking, running and jumping. This means that doing physical activities with your kid inspires your body to stay younger. As your child grows, they'll definitely challenge the limits of your endurance, and there's no actual way of keeping up with their little bodies of energy.

Fathering a child properly will lead to mind-blowing results that you will notice each day, and sometimes their growth can be seen after just a nap. One thing you want to constantly consider is that an inquisitive baby will always translate to an inquisitive toddler, and likely the same into childhood. This means that as you challenge your baby and teach them ways to be focused and dynamic, they will soon grow to challenge you in the same ways. As their brains grow, their mental capacity increases, and their curiosity skyrockets. As they get older, they are exposed to more reoccurring habits their parents may have or traditions that are often depicted in cartoons. As your toddler reaches three years old and beyond, you want to prepare yourself mentally to have your authority tested. Sharing an imagination with your toddler will sometimes have them test the boundaries of you being a parent and a guardian.

It's important to establish a form of verbal discipline with your child, where things can sometimes get out of hand as their personalities begin to develop more. Although children are smart, flexible and tactical, keep in mind that they are very ignorant of customs you may be used to, and are overall innocent in how they choose to approach problems. Rage and anger are very toxic responses to a toddler 'misbehaving' simply because there is no true learning in the process; the toddler may pick up on your habits of raising your voice when frustrated and reiterate that in high tension situations. This creates a horrible cycle for toddlers where they are confused as to why you are angry that they aren't expressing themselves properly, when you, the capable adult; are unable to keep your cool. Remember, this is an alien experience for your toddler and they will base their limitations off your words and actions. Connecting with your inner child will open up a level of trust for you from your toddler that is necessary for their growth.

Individuality is the beauty of life, but it often has us feeling alone, confused, and disconnected from others. Make sure your child has an early understanding in life that their father is a true teammate and protector rather than a judge; you never want your young child afraid to admit the truth before they even understand what it means to tell a lie. Another important fact in keeping your mind young is understanding that your toddler is much better at being a child than you are. This is because their inner child is also their outer self so they experience the hurdles of learning the meaning of life at a much higher rate than you do. While you've been through 12 grades of school and countless shifts of your job or career, it's altered your ability to understand simple concepts the same way your toddler can. Be extremely open to the idea that you can learn new things from your baby, despite them being so young and lacking in words. Showing your willingness to learn will most definitely rub off on your child, creating a safe space for them to accept the things you try to show them as important values for them to remember. By the time your toddler nears 4 years old; their brain is beginning to put words together into sentences at a very complex rate. Even though you've been through years of fatherhood, it will never stop amazing you just how intelligent your child is becoming. They'll begin to test their physical limits of balance and height while copying other children's mannerisms and phrases. This high level of absorbing information can be dangerous if you slack on connecting with your child and remaining a positive influence that can oppose the brazen things they do with a loving overtone.

Again, be sure to include repetition in all basic things like colors, shapes and letters, while staying on top of basic hygiene like taking baths/showers, brushing your teeth, and keeping your fingernails clean. Creating these habits on a repeated basis will help breed independence in your child. If you've truly given deep thought to fatherhood, you'll begin to hyper analyze many of the situations you face daily, and how you can help teach your toddler about them in kid-friendly ways. The biggest example I can give of this is teaching your toddler about money. No matter how connected to your inner child you become, your toddler will always notice you doing adult things like exchanging money for toys and groceries, or using the ATM to withdraw those green paper bills. As your child learns to formulate their thoughts and speak clearly, they'll begin to ask about money on their own. It's such a constant in our current lives that you'd have to be alarmed if your child doesn't ask about a dollar bill or coins at some point. It can be difficult explaining the language of money to a toddler, or what it means to have a currency in place. Essentially, we're trading our time and life force in exchange for a social representation of value. In this case, you really have to sit and think about what money is, what it was meant to be, and what it has become. Having to explain money to your child forces you to think deeply about it, then simplify it enough that they won't keep asking you follow up questions. This should be your approach to every single topic in life, from why and how it rains, to what a star is made out of.

Pay attention to the things your child gravitates towards too; besides the things you've introduced them to. As a father, you may have your toddler watch your favorite sports with you, or play with the hose while you wash your car on a sunny day; these are interests that a child may develop out of their need to connect and their sheer love for you. Whether they continue to enjoy cars or soccer into their adolescent years will depend completely on them, but the things they enjoy doing like dressing up, painting, or making music is the most important. Although you want to always push your child to be confident in trying new things, it's ideal to use your energy to motivate them in the areas they enjoy most. A great way to bond with and teach your child at the same time is reading to them often.

The entire concept of reading is intimidating and weird when you think about it. You see a bunch of symbols put together on a surface and they all represent different sounds and meanings. Together the symbols show ideas and thoughts about different people, places and things. You'll want to get your child used to the concept of seeing letters and processing those symbols as information because reading is a fundamental tool to survival as they grow up. As a bonus, this also gives you some quality time with your baby and allows you to blend both of your imaginations during storytime. Repetition in any field builds comfort, muscle memory, and releases dopamine hormones that make people happy for accomplishing tasks. This applies to your toddler as well, and you want to encourage them to unlock their talents by paying close attention to what they enjoy and investing in making sure your child gets to do it often. With all this mental, financial and spiritual work, you'll lose lots of sleep. It won't truly come back until much later on in your child's life, so it's important to cram this time with as much self-development as possible. As a father, you have to learn every day because you'll be expected to teach every day. Keep an understanding with your inner child so that you may empathize the battles your toddler is facing, and witness just how much you will grow as a man and human being from embracing this idea. Remember that your child is constantly learning and analyzing things every day. This means their brain is constantly studying YOU too, and how to survive in this world. It's figuring out "How do you get what you want? While also respecting other people's rights. How do you balance disagreements and collaborations?" A lot of times it may seem like your child is being sneaky or trying to manipulate your care for them. This is a natural process their mind goes through to try to understand what it can and can't do to achieve the satisfaction of your toddler's young desires. Be committed to being a kind, understanding leader and try not to push negative intentions on your child by assuming or projecting that they're mentally capable of trying to manipulate you with ill intent.

A toddler can be as clever as an adult, but they are never as intentional or aware as an adult and it's important to never assume this when approaching disciplining your child. Calling your child things like "bad" "rude" or "crazy" may seem like harmless gestures in the beginning, but over time it may lead you to responding aggressively or being unconsciously viewing these behavioral traits as something you can't necessarily correct. Reassuring your child of their strengths and rewarding them for doing a good job or giving effort is always a good thing to do. As important as it is for a child to hear they are smart or going about something the right way; it's equally important to find a way to stress the importance of trying hard to succeed. Studies show that children who are told they are smart will have high expectations of themselves but respond badly to failure, leaning away from things that they might fail to avoid a challenge. Toddlers can get addicted to chasing praise, which shrinks their ability to first be wrong, learn from it then becomes better. This is a sensitive area for a lot of fathers because they have been raised to chase praise and avoid challenges. Use this moment to take a look in the mirror and ask if this applies to you as well. Letting your child know that they've succeeded because they try hard, rather than succeeding because they're naturally smart, will build a sort of mental process that allows them to be resilient from a very early age. Helping your child build all these new characteristics while being engaged in their everyday lives will give you the perfect chance to grow yourself and sharpen your integrity. This is the beauty of fatherhood because as they say, you're a man once, but twice a child.

Chapter 6:
Mind Magic

As I stated before, parents are superheroes. You're responsible for the city of emotions, feelings and curiousness that is your child. The perks of being a superhero is being Super. Like the saying goes "with great power comes great responsibility". And the only way to master this power is to identify your power and practice using it. As a father, your great magic is the ability to read minds and see the future. As the parent that did not give birth or share blood with your baby, it's your responsibility to create a unique bond with your child that mirrors a sort of friendship. Even as your baby learns to speak, they cannot understand or emote themselves fully and that's where your magic steps in. As you know by now, studying your child's likes and dislikes; subtle changes in attitude, and how they demand attention, are all ways to better understand their growing personality. By doing this, you'll literally be able to read their minds in a sense. By paying attention to patterns especially, you'll gain the perspective of a best friend finishing their sentences. You'll be able to tell when they're afraid or nervous and what elements of a task discourage them specifically. This all will allow you to gauge your child's confidence, self-control, and attention span at a very early age, and build on healthy behavior while correcting bad behavior. What is bad behavior for a child? It's hard to decide on what's right or wrong morally, but what's most important is what traits will best help your child survive in the world for as long as they live.

This brings me to your next and even more divine superpower. The ability to see the future. Both parents share this power, and it's vital that they work together on using it to help their innocent child. Have you ever heard of the Dunedin Study? It is a scientific project where researchers studied the many stages of psychology in 1,000 humans from the start of their lives to the age of 40. This groundbreaking research has led to a plethora of respected and published discoveries in how early childhood is linked to the success, health and stability in adults. The study breaks down all child personalities into 5 different branches. While it states that children that display confidence or are well-adjusted have a higher chance of growing up to be successful adults, it also states that shy kids or children with lesser levels of self-control turn out to have harder lives; and are even linked to criminal activity and sickness. I encourage you to look up this study and gain a better understanding of how people are analyzed in early childhood because all of the first worlds acknowledge its findings.

To really hit home how this knowledge unlocks telling the future, we need to speak more here on understanding your child's self-control. Around 24 months, your toddler is beginning to show signs of many motor skills and verbal functions. This is as soon as you can start looking for early signs of your child's persona, paying attention to how they respond to ending TV or playtime, snacks being finished, or their favorite activities coming to an end. Understand this is NOT a test, simply observation so you can better understand your child's natural instinct. The reason I'm so harsh on self-control is that it seems to be the most constant factor to human success no matter the upbringing. Self-control in your child can reflect their financial status, marital status, educational status and health upkeep as an adult. Having self-regulation means being able to control your actions in situations where emotional responses release adrenaline in your body. Some people get angry and start saying things they don't mean, disabling their ability to think clearly. This is why responding to tantrums with aggression isn't a healthy means of discipline. The most basic way to help your child with their self-control is detaching them from environments that trigger their confusion and more importantly, working on telling them to take a deep breath. Toddlers may have cuddle toys or pacifiers that they are attached to that can calm them down... but it's best to work on techniques that will transcend their age, as habits like pacifiers are fool's gold and can ruin dental structural growth as a child grows past two years old. Teaching your child how to stop and take a deep breath when things get overwhelming can spark a simple change in the way their brain processes feelings and how to approach situations. I've also seen some parents construct entire "Zen areas" for their children to calm down. It includes actually researching calming methods, but it's worth looking into with Mom. Consistency is key, so repeating the teachings and having discipline in being the leader your baby needs is the goal.

As I say with anything else, take this opportunity to apply these moments to yourself too. Try to get a perspective of what kind of person you are, and what kind of child you were. Were you Confident, or Bashful? Did you get in where you fit in during most situations? Did you lack self-control or maybe were very introverted and keep to yourself? Grasping this will help you tremendously in growing as a father and a man while also mastering your self-control in life. Figuring yourself out while figuring out your child is challenging when you're expected to apply information that you're just learning for yourself. This is why research and planning early are so crucial, even if you're a superhero. Once you've got a better perspective on your child's personality, you'll be able to see the future well into their teenage years and understand what traits to encourage or which to help them correct. If your child isn't born yet, the only thing you can wish for is a healthy baby. Once you've achieved that, it's up to you to keep them happy and in a constant environment of care, attention and respect. As a father, you should be the epicenter of fun, wisdom and challenges. Always push your child to be brave and confident in trying new things while teaching them the dangers and rewards of their actions. While you want to be hands-on and tender, you need to leave plenty of space for your child to be independent and solve issues on their own. It's surprisingly swift how well a child's brain works, and after seeing or feeling you do something a few times, they may be able to do the task themselves. The process of a child connecting a thought or a want into a calculated physical series of actions to achieve it is a BIG DEAL. Allow your child to tackle these small challenges as much as possible and REWARD THEM FOR TRYING HARD.

Words of encouragement are an emotional boost; while your child may be a genius and impel you to tell them how smart they are, it's better to reinforce that their reason for success was their effort. If you can master being this great-big-brother-leader-dad, you can lead with love. This puts your child in a space where being in your energy is so warm and inspiring that they will dislike ever being in your bad favor. Mind control, maybe? It's what happens when mommy is having trouble and she says "I'm going to call daddy!" chances are that child doesn't want you upset with their behavior. If you do the work, you'll notice your child having very adult-like self-reflecting moments on how they've disappointed you and in what ways they can be better. It's truly a mental magic that will set the building blocks for a lifelong task of raising your offspring.

You're now the most important man in the universe to someone, and you owe it to them to consider EVERYTHING, being the superhero, you're meant to be. Using your magic powers leaves you better equipped to deal with everyday hurdles as a father and also preparing your child for the modern world. Speaking of the modern world, try your best to never let the weight of your adult life push you to take out stress on your young child. Your feelings are temporary and low vibrational, while kids are delicate and impressionable. This is more important than you think because one irrational moment can trigger a trauma in your child for a long time. You know the joke that says "you can't tell your girlfriend she's speaking too much because she'll never speak again"? That joke about women being too sensitive is a great example of behavior that can scar a child. Children ARE sensitive, so telling a child they're speaking too much can literally create a mental process that will stop them from talking even in environments where they need to be vocal. Watch what you say at all times and use your powerful mind to think before you engage with your child in tense situations. Take a deep breath.

Although there are many links to early child development and adulthood, there is one factor of your child that can be molded to help them succeed no matter how naturally rebellious or shy they may seem. That factor is Creativity. Even if you aren't much of a creative guy yourself, as a Father, now is the best time to unlock your creative side, my brother. I've mentioned the word earlier and we need to revisit it because creativity builds perspective; perspective is everything. It's time to pick up a pencil and draw something original; brush your teeth with your less dominant hand then try your hand at putting together a poem. If you already consider yourself as creative, then that's great as well. The point here is to find a way to identify, encourage, and stimulate your child's creativity. We live in a realm where Order and Chaos coexist at the same time to create the beauty of life. The human body is complex yet simple, made up of basic elements like air, water, chalk and coal. We're filled with wonders too, from quarks in our protons to genome communities in our gut. The true essence of our existence, however, is our brain. Our brain transmits our consciousness while using our senses to understand what's going on around it, and using our vital organs to keep it energized and absorb nutrients from outside sources. Basically, our body is a house and engine for our brains to exist somewhat peacefully. What I'm trying to say is, we ARE our brain. It's important to make sure your child knows that their brain is their most beautiful and important feature. Creativity can be a touchy subject because it's hard to measure how creative someone is. Children are the cleanest minds on the planet and have the opportunity to approach common situations in new ways. Don't prohibit your child from testing their limits and ideas by enforcing social norms on them, because their creativity might be outside your wired way of seeing things. The greatest gift a human can give to the world is a new idea that can change the way we do things, so it's ideal to keep your child on course to grow into an innovative adult.

With my own child, I noticed her creativity very early on in her life when she would play with toys in her crib. As a toddler, she would use ANYTHING around her to create whatever she imagined. One day she plucked dried rose petals off flowers I bought for her mom. She placed the petals in a hallowed building block toy she has and said it was a cup of applesauce. At the time, she was playing a daycare for her plushie toys and even used a wooden worm toy as a spoon to feed them. In this example, there are a plethora of traits you can look for in your child to see if there's creative energy you should build on. Things like giving personality traits to their toys, using toys outside of their original intended purpose, and incorporating everyday items into their play with a new approach; all things to look out for to tell just how naturally creative your child is capable of being.

A playful, happy child can stimulate their own creativity at a much higher level than kids who are scolded for fearlessly displaying their own personalities. Be sure to include discipline to learning in everything they do, creating a healthy balance of building creativity and intelligence. Simple things like asking what the first letter of a word they've just said is, and saying the sound the letter makes, can help stimulate their mind when done in repetition. It's easier said than done, but never get lax on enforcing your teaching habits because you find your child excelling beyond their age. The reason I stress repetition is that the young brain is powerful and stores tons of information not even directed at the child, so it's easy for them to forget basic knowledge like the names of colors they may have seemed to have down packed. Fully explaining things to kids can come back to bite as they get older and continue to grow a critical thinking mindset, yet it's still a wise choice to push them past their emotions of fear and nervousness with a soft approach and fully explaining why they may be overreacting sometimes. It's good to let children know early that no one's judgment of them defines who they are. As kids begin to understand themselves and have an idea of how they want to be perceived, they'll begin to fully experience embarrassment but won't know exactly how to explain it. There'll be moments where they're both excited and afraid to try something leading to disappointment in themselves. It's up to you Dad, as the adult who has experienced this many times before, to explain to them what they're feeling and why it isn't the end of the world. Knowing your child is important here because like I've said before, one wrong approach can send them into an emotional shell. This is a good time to use your creativity and work with mom on creating systems to calm your child beyond simple breathing techniques and timeout corners. I know fatherhood can be staggering but just remember, take a deep breath.

Chapter 7:
Doing the Hard Work

The saying goes "It's a man's world", yes...but being a good man is a very hard job. Understanding how to be the best man YOU can be is fundamental to being a good father. Building on yourself as a man is already a lifelong effort, especially with all the distractions and incorrect traditions self-imposed on men. It's very difficult to grow when you view the things that hold you back instead as strong points in your development simply because they hide your vulnerability and mask you from doing the hard yet true work. This gives yourself the impression that you're as tough as a man needs to be to survive being the head of household in an ever-changing world. It's true, there's no room for dramatic men in this world. Consider that no matter how 'open' of a man a woman may want, it's possible to emotionally lose your partner by being more sensitive or unsure of your direction than the next man. It's important to find the balance within yourself and close the gap on emotional intelligence between men and their counterparts; yet appear stern and calculated. They say silence is golden, and it's a good trait to master. Always communicate but don't get caught up in the power struggle of needing to be right.

As a leader, you're always going to face an opposing voice...but the first step to convincing someone you're serious is by trusting your own vision and never allowing someone else to detour you as a man. Radiating confidence will always rub off on your partner like it does your child. And if it doesn't, they aren't much of a partner at all. Regardless of your situation, remain reasonable and be a man in the best way that helps your family. It's always good to know the root of your issues as a man, but embrace being the leader of your family. Take your time and move at a pace that doesn't overwhelm you, but learn to hurry up. As much as it is important to get aware of your feminine energy, it's much more detrimental to grow within your masculinity. It's hard work keeping up with so many things on such a deep perspective, but ignorance is bliss.

I cannot explain to you the essence of being a man in this world, and the role of every man is different depending on their situation. Your role as a father primarily remains the same. Mastering your role as Daddy and mastering your role as a man goes hand in hand; being a better man opens the discipline needed to be a better Father. A lot of people take pride in the fact that they haven't changed much since they were young, signifying that they've "remained true to self" in a sense. If there's ever been a time to kill that vibe, it's now. Connecting with your inner child doesn't mean you get to ever be childish. For the first time in life, you aren't only responsible for yourself and owe it to your child to transform from a wanderer going through the journey of life, into a guru who can understand anything well enough to teach and protect their offspring. A lot of people are making the effort to change, but the true goal is growth. It's good to know the difference between change and growth. Change is a common demand, a quick fix by always keeping something in mind and making an effort to apply it to your mindset. Change is difficult, because it's superficial. It's full of empty promises to yourself and that's why people say "you can't change overnight". Growth on the other hand, is an organic process that starts with understanding a trait you have is actually a flaw. Admitting that a pattern you display is not a strong point to who you are is the first step in achieving something greater than change. It allows you to analyze who you are, and really become disgusted with issues about yourself that you're inspired to work on. Growth differs from change because it requires a painful sense of awareness that turns into productive confidence. Rather than wasting your energy on giving effort the wrong way, aim to grow. Men tend to try and change out of spite, shutting up their partners. It's unhealthy and stunts communication with everyone in your life. Instead, consider other people's perspectives and ask yourself if the criticism can help you be better. From there you can decide if you prefer the person you are now, or if you can work on eliminating habits that interrupts harmony in your life. People never change, they can only grow, which brings changes; poetic really. The people who aren't always around to witness you grow may say that you've changed, but it's important for you to personally know the difference.

That being said, fathers need to grow from being money hungry survivors to becoming efficient and tactical planners. If you haven't already, learn how to shop efficiently like using grocery papers to find sales with the intention of saving money. It's crucial to learn how to drive and teach yourself how to cook better, so try using online recipes. No matter the gender of your first child, learn about doing hair and different hair textures. Get yourself a plant or two and learn how to care for a living thing by following routines and supplying resources. It's wise to study some form of carpentry or building as well since at minimum you'll be putting cribs and car seats together. We live in the age of information, where a surplus of instructions and new ideas can be found on YouTube or a Google search bar. You'll have to apply yourself to thinking ahead and keeping yourself busy with building on healthy habits as a man. I know I've said many times that parenthood is void of sleep, but you'll need to find a way to stabilize your sleeping patterns once your infant gets older. When we sleep, an interesting chemical reaction goes on in our brains. While the rest of our organs essentially go into low maintenance mode, our brain has the time to now take care of itself. Science has found that our brains go through a process where fluids flush the mental clutter from our minds, removing old neurons and the wasteful thoughts they've produced from firing off electrical signals in your mind all day. While this flush happens, your brain is also processing the information you gathered for the day, and comparing it to items or words in past stored memories to sort out their importance. Some scientists believe this is what "dreams" are, glimpses of you seeing your brain put things together and store or release the information. This means that sleep correlates with memory, and more importantly keeping your brain fresh to make swift, wise decisions. No matter what your role as a man is, the most common situation you will be faced with is being leaned on to make decisions. Make sure you own this responsibility and do the research to put yourself in the best position to know what to do next.

An essential trait for any man to have is Foresight. Having foresight is similar to your superpower, and it means you're able to predict something that's going to happen. That takes focus, planning, and most importantly, confidence in the idea that you will succeed in whatever it is you set out to do. Uncertainty is very normal whenever a person attempts a new thing or enters any sort of commitment, so it's a process you should get used to overcoming. If you can trust in the process and bet on yourself, you should have a hard time failing. Even if you do fail at something, you have to remember that failure is way more common than success. A lot of people don't share their failures because they haven't gained enough self-awareness to be vulnerable about it. You don't necessarily have to share your failures, but make sure you don't get too down on yourself because of it. Failure just means you gave effort to something and learned a lesson to apply to your new approach. It's a process and a part of success, so embrace it. As the leader of your family, your mistakes may be highlighted or blown out of proportion, because your partner won't be able to clearly see your goal. If she does, it's a blessing; but never expects it. Using this confidence that you will get the job done is as good as telling the future. You WILL make things happen, therefore the efforts you show will be the best you can give. Paying attention to detail and taking time to research what's going on in the world is another part of having foresight. It's important to have as a leader and a provider; you'll be able to see things coming in the real world that may affect your financial situations. Avoiding obstacles before they happen can better secure your mind and your partner's confidence in you as the father of their child. All of humanity seems to be raised with flaws, but this book is specifically for all my brothers; the Men. Men in most western societies have been raised with many, many flaws. When you're raising someone to live in a competitive society, you tend to feed them traits that give them a little more edge and drive, a little less compassion and more toughness. It may be all you have to offer too, being raised in such a competitive environment yourself. Most men are raised to be leaders, and rightfully so.

I've brought it up before, so let's take a look at the word "Leader" for a second, and fully understand what's normally expected from them. As a leader, you're responsible for the people that "follow" you. It's your job to make the tough decisions while making sure everyone you lead feels just as important as you are to the operation. When facing danger, a leader is expected to reassure his people that their fears, confusion, or uncertainty are natural, but overreactions. A leader is supposed to make his people feel secure. The issue in this leadership role is the humanity it strips away from a man. To make someone feel like their fears and uncertainty will never happen, a person has to feel that way himself. This often puts men in space where they feel like they cannot reveal that they too have fears, or that he is in a safe space to process uncertainty. This can spiral a man down a dark road, making him bitter towards parts of his family, or feeling unappreciated for dealing with (internal) situations (no one is aware of). This is a hard topic to speak with women on because they feel like it's strictly internal, an issue that men bring upon ourselves entirely. They've always grown up in a space where they're expected to be dramatic and emotionally free, so breaking down the layers of your leadership role to your woman can and will be tough. Ultimately, she doesn't have to care about it because part of your job is making her feel equal...so she won't really enjoy conversations where you speak of yourself as a "Leader" or sort of King, even if the dynamic feels true and upheld by her. Truthfully, she's a leader in her own right too, and has her own daily issues. From trying to be a leader in a competitive and unfair world, men often end up aggressive, emotionally detached and regressed in forms of communication. The best remedy for this is by wanting the best for yourself. Don't get caught up on proving anyone wrong, or being motivated by negative things. You owe it to your child and everyone in your support system to continuously work on being better.

An ability that most men lack, myself included, is knowing how to Listen. It's funny to read this since humans seemingly always hear what someone is saying, but allowing someone to complete their thoughts and have an open ear to speak to is critical when being a leader. We tend to boomerang conversations back to ourselves to display a sense of empathy to a subject or have the urge to try and fix a situation by offering advice. Even with our kids, we may jump to their aide with our fatherly instincts and try to give them our best perspective on how to avoid mistakes. These are examples of being a bad listener. With your partner and others, be a silent listener and practice taking in what others are talking about without fulfilling your urge to add input. With your child, never cast judgment or know-it-all advice before you even let them express what's on their mind. It may seem like a simple practice to overlook, but if you glance deep into the mirror you might find this flaw in yourself as a man. It's okay! You've got plenty of time to understand what qualities you need to work on; as long as you're willing to learn.

Once you become open to the idea of being a better man, you can approach your specific flaws properly. Always remember that our counterparts are raised in a specific way as well and it has its side effects too, so many of the things they align themselves with backfire as well. Everyone has room to unlearn because no one is perfect, and you should always give your partner room to make mistakes as well. I know she's an angel to you, but she's actually just human. If you're going to lead, lead by example and give her the space to figure herself out the same way you need space to figure yourself out as well. Focus on doing your own hard work rather than criticizing others.

From the day of the pregnancy test, during mom's pregnancy and your time raising a newborn, everything you know about being a man may all go out the window because of how sensitive a time it is for your family. As we discussed, your partner is going through massive hormonal changes and suddenly there's a bundle of joy in your lives that need constant care and focus. It can be overwhelming for sure, but I've put together several basic and specific questions to ask yourself as a man even before becoming a father. These questions are designed to stimulate thought and give you an idea of how seriously you'll have to plan your steps if you want to be the best Father you can be:

What examples of good parenting do I remember from my own Father and other male guardians?

Do I have a plan to afford essentials like diapers and wipes as well as proper shelter for my child?

How will I make time to be there for my pregnant partner as well as the newborn while my partner recovers from labor?

What kind of person do I want my child to see when they look at me?

What kind of father do I want to be? Can I be a leader while showing compassion and understanding?

Do I understand that fatherhood differs vastly from motherhood and the different responsibilities coming together to raise a child?

Am I allowing the sensitive words and actions of my partner to influence the love and respect I show them?

Do I have a healthy support system? Do I trust my immediate family and close friends to be a village that helps feed positivity to my child?

Am I displaying good decision-making skills and communicating my victories or losses?

Am I taking my finances seriously by creating a plan and budget to secure my family's needs?

Do I understand the seriousness of the now eternal bond I have with the mother of my child?

Do I give emotional and spiritual security? Do I allow my partner to be happy or angry and express her feelings in ways safest for her?

Do I understand that as a man my role is to take the blame for things going right or wrong? Do I realize that by taking the blame instead of debating rationality, I can move on quickly to finding solutions?

Do I understand that as a father I owe my child for bringing it into the world and owe the mother for risking her life to give birth?

Can I be a very engaged father with my child despite any romantic issues with my partner?

Why did this child choose me to be his/her father in this world and what benefits can I bring to his/her life's purpose?

Do I acknowledge that the world belongs to the youth and I must play my part in treating my child as an important part of the future?

Do I take the time to truly sit with my feelings and understand where my different emotions stem from? Do I exhibit behavior that shows love and vulnerability with myself before expecting love from others?

Do I take accountability for the damages I've caused and how it may affect the interactions I have with my partner or others in my life?

How would I want my child to speak about me at my funeral? Am I living up to what I envision?

If you'd like, write down your answers to the questions so that you can put your response into the universe; own your strengths or faults and manifest being better. I'm sure you're already doing a fantastic job in life and may be more prepared for fatherhood than you think, but never get complacent. As I said earlier, fathers often get caught in a cycle of leaving motherly roles entirely to their partner. It seems ideal but the problem is that men often view a lot of basic things as "motherly roles". I mean simple things like keeping a copy of your child's birth certificate. Believe it or not, a lot of fathers don't even remember their child's exact birthday especially when they have more than one child. At the bare minimum, a father should understand how to enroll their child into school and extracurricular programs, their dentist and doctors, blood type, and ESPECIALLY the allergies their child may have. Knowing your child's social security number or having access to it at all times is a cherry on top. I hope this doesn't seem like a lot, because it is the least you can do as a father. Even if mom isn't sharp in all those departments, don't use your partner's parenting methods as a benchmark for what's acceptable for you as a father. Remember, the theme is to approach everything with importance, and be better. As you grow more as a man and a father, the answers to the questions above may change. It's a good idea to return to these questions if you happen to have another child, and compare your growth as a Father by reviewing your old and new answers. When you're doing the hard work, it's rewarding to acknowledge and celebrate your growth.

Conclusion

So, how does it feel brother? You're the center of the world and the last in line at the same time. Parenting is a weird, beautiful complexity that we often overlook until it smacks us in the face. A good father will go through countless stressful encounters and will be tasked with slaying many beasts. Every small and large battle against parenting obstacles will exercise your ability to be better. While the world may seem too vast for you to ever be important, fatherhood is a world where you mean the most; the sharpest blade. Don't forget you have a team with you for every battle now too. Consider how your every move will affect them, how protected they will be, and how available you keep yourself to help them when in need. Raising your child is a task, but the more human they become, the more they can help you grow and be a useful asset to your team. If you're into dungeons and fantasy, then consider yourself the Knight of your team. You wear the armor and lift the heavy weaponry to strike down the goblins of hardship. Tough skin and physical labor are expected from you when the financial dragons roar. Mom is more of the Healer of the team. Her power is just as important as yours, in a different dynamic. She's there to understand your hardships and be considerate; nurse your wounds. As you protect her, it gives her the time to witness your battles, understand where you've been hit, and be sensitive to your pain. When loved correctly, a woman can become a powerful healer. It's not her job to heal you, but it's in her nature...make sure you help her unlock that. When her light is strong enough, it's even more powerful than your blades (They refer to this as "divine femininity" and you should look it up to help understand women better). Your child is the last member of your immediate team, and they serve as the Magician. Their powers are strong and mystical; take tons of practice, focus, and dedication. When your child receives a healthy and protected environment to work their magic, they can be a fundamental piece to your team. As they say, people with kids stay younger longer. Seeing your child discover themselves on their own will be a joy to watch and leave you in awe at all times. Make sure you're there as much as you can be to absorb it all. Their magic will always make your sword stronger. Working together as a party, your family can accomplish anything you want.

If you've done the work, you'll have established a friendship with your child that is irreplaceable. For the first time besides maybe your parents, you'll have crafted a connection with another human being who will help you grow for the rest of your life. Your child will be able to have tough conversations with you and give constructive criticism on the overall direction and outcome of your life from a unique perspective. If the love is pure, your child will be able to tell you things about yourself that other people may have left you alone for. Your selfishness, stubbornness, unwillingness to change and your overreactions are all reasons why your friendships and relationships might have fallen out or never grown. Most times, people distance themselves from you rather than going through the trouble of telling you things you may not want to hear. As men, we tend to lean on our egos, seeing ourselves in high regard based on the vision we have for ourselves. This can sometimes make us combative and difficult to speak with about real issues, especially if you're underdeveloped with your ability to self-reflect or have self-control. If you're reading this, then you're already working on being better in those departments. As a man, there isn't much room in society for your flaws, but as a father? There's still plenty of hope! If you've been a consistent parent and done the work correctly, you'll build a stern bond with your child and won't take offense to their criticisms. You both will be truthful and warm with each other, receptive and respectful of one another's opinions. Having access to this sort of relationship as a man is fundamental to working past the things about yourself that hold you back in life. The love will be unconditional and organic because you've invested your mind, body, and heart into being a great father. It isn't your child's responsibility to help you become a better person, but rather a miraculous gift you've unlocked through dynamic, healthy parenting.

From before the day your child was born, you took your new role in life seriously and made a vow to prepare yourself. You've taken the time to prioritize the meaning of life and better yourself as a survivor and teacher in the mental, emotional, spiritual & financial areas of your life. You've learned just how drastic the changes your partner is going through are, and how much effort and work you need to do to go through your own rebirth into a parent. You've taken the time to have a long look in the mirror and instill more compassion, sensitivity, and understanding in your heart. From the moment your child is born, you've poured nothing but love and patience into them while bettering the environment around you. That is fatherhood. Displaying a man who is dynamic enough to be loving and caring while also precise and determined is the key to fatherhood. A great example of this is the late Kobe Bryant. In his craft of basketball, he was a psychotic murderer on the court. There was no weak point in his game, his leadership and will to never give up was evident in every move he made. I once saw Kobe have his elbow dislocated on a play; without going to the locker room he had one of the team trainers pop his arm back into place and he returned to the game without missing a play. Just an unreal testament to how seriously he takes what he loves. Off the court, Bryant was a phenomenal father to his daughters and a great husband to mom. That duality is what made him loved worldwide and accepted for his flaws. It's that simple. The goal is not to be perfect, because no one is perfect. The goal is to be the best you, without setting limitations on yourself. Tell yourself that you can achieve whatever it is you want, and then prove it to yourself. As the saying goes, don't talk about it; be about it. It's right to manifest your plans by saying them out loud, but never say something you aren't going to do. Perfection is subjective because good and bad traits differ depending on the mindset a person has. You will never be perfect because of this, so the most important thing is to be proud of yourself. Be able to accept when your flaws are pointed out because you've already pointed them out within yourself. If you can understand that you, your best friend, can call yourself out and still love yourself... you'll have an easier time understanding that people can say pretty hurting things while still coming from a good place. Don't waste time wishing someone would be more sensitive or attentive to how you communicate, but rather fill yourself with principles that allow you to have no shame in you always needing to grow.

Men indeed operate based on ego and concepts the world has given us. For example, we don't want anyone to know our partner may have cheated on us, because of what it may imply about ourselves. Most women will tell each other that a man cheating has nothing to do with her, and actually shows his immaturity and inability to communicate his desires. On the other end, most women will also support the idea that a woman cheated on a man because of something that he probably isn't doing. Rest assured brothers, this isn't the case. It's true for us too that a woman cheating on us has nothing to do with us, and has everything to do with her immaturity and lack of accountability. Even the obsession with getting even or being petty is deemed dangerous in men but acceptable for women. My point is, love your pride but work on breaking down your Ego. Things like mental health, financial assistance, and sexual displeasure are often things men hide because society seemingly flips the reasoning back on men, from all angles. Men are easily funneled into this mindset because of ego, and learning never to let anyone see you cry or seem broken down. Having good people in your corner who support you breaking out of social norms is important, but you won't even be able to surround yourself with these kinds of people if you can't first realize that your ego binds you to these self-destructive ideals. Love yourself and understand that life is hard, and despite what you may see going on in society; we all need help. We all take losses and it's important to own them so we can grow from them. Women say that men get their hearts broken in junior high school and never love again; in most cases they're right. Open yourself to being a beautiful person beyond your ego or whatever image of yourself you prefer the world to see. If you've been working on yourself at all, you'll know what I mean... those embarrassing thoughts you have that you coach yourself out of thinking about? OWN THEM. This is part of who you are, and processing those emotions without considering what the outside world may project on you will help you grow immensely. Growth is the goal.

As your newborn grows into an infant, and your infant grows into a toddler, then later into childhood and their teenage years; never stop seeking out new ways to grow as a parent. You'll build your mold as a father even though your baby and their personality will be ever-changing. You'll know how you discipline, how you reward, how you balance fun and learning, how you instill life lessons, and how you express your feelings with your child. As they grow older, you'll learn these very things about your child as well, but more importantly, you'll learn that your child is a human being who will make mistakes and have secrets. There will ALWAYS be new hurdles, and I want you to be prepared for that brother. Make sure you take lots of pictures and cherish the little moments because, after a while, time flies, and your bundle of joy will become a hyperactive teenager. Fatherhood is an endless journey so I won't be able to fit all the advice possible into one book. I myself don't have all the answers or even half the answers... but I do know how fundamentally important the first five years of your child's life is. I do know how important being a father is, and just how devastating it can be not to have an active father in a child's life. I know you love your child, and you want the best for them. I know you're an amazing father. Do you know how I know? Because you're *here*, with me. We've had this intimate conversation about life, parenthood, and manhood. You've embraced the idea of needing help and you've kept an open mind; keep practicing this. Keep reading, researching, googling, asking, failing, learning, succeeding, and embracing whatever lesson you can out of every situation. If you want to be a great parent, you'll need to remain diligent, stay sharp, and try your best to stay young and keep connected with your child. Be a team with not just Mom, but her immediate family, as much as you may be with your own family. The more people that are involved in embracing your child with love, the easier it will be for your baby to feel safe in this world. The easier YOU are to love, the easier it will be for others to translate that same love to your child. Not everyone is blessed with that type of teamwork, but if you can secure it for yourself and your child; work for it.

Nothing in life worth having will come easy, but creating the right bond with your kid will be an irreplaceable source of love. Helping them become the best person they can be (even better than you) will forever be referred to as a "thankless job" but trust me, your child will thank you in abundance; over and over. Being proud of your child is a feeling I can barely put into words, and experiencing the surprise and joy of seeing their talents and abilities grow will be unforgettable memories in your life that you'll constantly be proud of.

You'll pay less attention to yourself aging as you see them grow smarter, taller, faster, and stronger. Fatherhood is a blessing. It welcomes you to a world where you can no longer be selfish or pay attention to only your benefit. The paradox of this development is that it will in fact push you to be more successful than you ever have been. It will challenge you to push past your limits, and work much harder for yourself than you ever could, by yourself. You're the leader and a warrior, a gentle and kind father who uses love and understanding to be a better parent. Thank you for reading and embracing my message, all the way until the end. If you keep practicing discipline while applying these dad habits to everyday life, there are no limits to what your family can become. Good luck with everything my brother; I know you've got this covered, Dad.

VOCABULARY

Important   - of great significance or value; likely to have a profound effect on success, survival, or well-being (mentioned **65** times).

Parent   - a caregiver of the offspring in one's own species (mentioned **90** times).

Learn   - to gain or acquire knowledge of or skill in (something) by study, experience, or being taught (mentioned **76** times).

Mind   - the element of a person that enables them to be aware of the world and their experiences, to think, and to feel; the faculty of consciousness and thought (mentioned **56** times).

Love   - an intense feeling of deep affection (mentioned **43** times).

9 781646 206582